8/00

22.50

THE KINGDOM OF BENIN

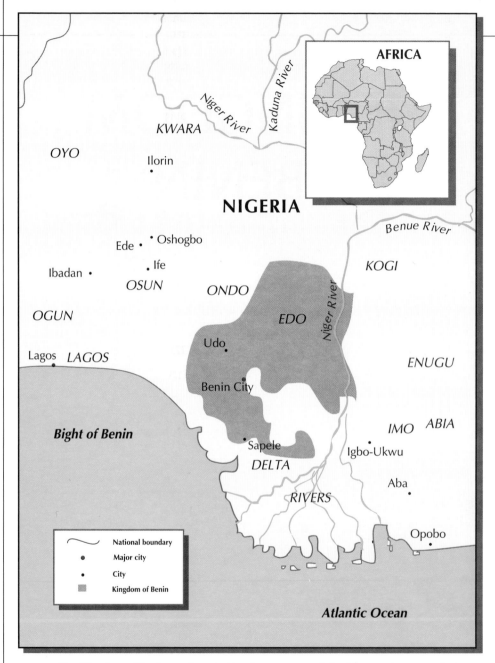

The Kingdom of Benin was founded by the ancestors of the Edo people, many of whom live in southern Nigeria today.

~African Civilizations~

THE KINGDOM OF BENIN

Dominique Malaquais, Ph.D.

A First Book

Franklin Watts
A Division of Grolier Publishing
New York / London / Hong Kong / Sydney
Danbury, Connecticut

To Tyler Holland-Ashford, my godson.

Photographs copyright ©: Cover Photograph: The Metropolitan Museum of
Art/The Michael C. Rockefeller Memorial Collection; Werner Forman
Archive: p. 10; Phyllis Galembo: pp. 12, 54; From the collection of Robin B.
Martin, currently on loan to The Brooklyn Museum of Art: p. 14; Werner
Forman Archive/Museum for Volkerkunde, Berlin/Art Resource: p. 16; Erich
Lessing/Art Resource: p. 19; Library of Congress/Corbis: p. 22; Werner
Forman Archive/Courtesy Entwistle Gallery, London/Art Resource: pp. 26,
38; Art Resource/The Bridgeman Art Library, British Museum, London: p.
28; Courtesy of Joseph Nevadomsky: p. 32; Eliot Elisofon Photographic
Archives/National Museum of African Art: pp. 36, 39; 1991 The Metropoli-
tan Museum of Art: p. 41; Frank Khoury/National Museum of African Art:
p. 42; Werner Forman Archive/British Museum, London (Museum of
Mankind)/Art Resource: p. 44; Werner Forman Archive/Morton Simpson
Collection, New York/Art Resource: p. 45; Werner Forman Archive/University
Museum, Philadelphia: p. 46; Trip/J. Highet/Viesti Associates, Inc.: p. 50;
Joseph Nevadomsky: p. 53.

Library of Congress Cataloging-in-Publication Data

Malaquais, Dominique.
    The kingdom of Benin / Dominique Malaquais. — 1st ed.
      p.   cm. — (A first book)   (African civilizations)
    Includes bibliographical references and index.
    Summary: A survey of the history and culture of the West African
kingdom of Benin that flourished after Eweka I became king about
1300 and fathered a dynasty that still exists today.
    ISBN 0-531-20279-8
    1. Benin (Kingdom)—History—Juvenile literature. 2. Bini (African
people)—History—Juvenile literature. [1. Benin (Kingdom)—History.]
I. Title. II. Series. III. Series: African civilizations.
DT515.9.B37M25   1998
966.9'301—dc21   97-37373
                                                           CIP
                                                            AC

Copyright © 1998 by The Rosen Publishing Group, Inc.
All rights reserved. Published simultaneously in Canada
Printed in the United States of America
1 2 3 4 5 6 7 8 9 10 R 05 04 03 02 01 00 99 98

CONTENTS

INTRODUCTION

Of all the kingdoms founded in Africa over the centuries, the Kingdom of Benin (pronounced ben-EEN) is one of the most famous. Located in West Africa in what is today southern Nigeria, the kingdom was founded in the 1200s. Its first inhabitants and rulers belonged to the *Edo* ethnic group, a people known for their skills as farmers and builders. Initially a small community, it quickly grew into a kingdom. By the 1400s, when Europeans first visited the region, Benin had become a mighty state.

The capital of the kingdom was the town of Edo. Today this town is called Benin City. It is located about 30 miles (48 km) inland from the Atlantic Ocean, in a low-lying region of tropical rain forests, rivers, and streams.

At the height of its power, the Kingdom of Benin extended far north of Benin City. To the east, it reached as far as the Niger River. To the west, it stretched into lands controlled by Yoruba monarchs—kings and queens who ruled over city-states renowned for their wealth and mighty armies. At one time, the kingdom reached as far as Lagos—today one of Africa's largest cities—170 miles (272 km) west of Benin City.

Although most of Benin's inhabitants were Edo, the kingdom included people from many different backgrounds. Some of its citizens were Yoruba; others were Igala, Igbo, Ijaw, Ishan, and Itsekiri—all peoples of southern Nigeria who had come together under the rule of Benin's leaders. This diversity played an important role in shaping the kingdom, giving it a unique character and complexity.

Many of the kingdom's inhabitants lived outside the capital, in villages governed by councils of male elders. Most of its people were farmers. Though daily existence in the villages had little to do with life in the capital, strong political and economic ties linked each outlying village to Benin City, which was the heart and soul of the kingdom.

1 THE GROWTH OF THE KINGDOM

The early history of the Kingdom of Benin is something of a mystery. Two sources of knowledge provide us with information about its origins and days of glory. The first source is data gathered by archaeologists, scientists who study the way humans lived a long time ago. The second is Edo oral history—accounts from the past that the Edo people have passed from generation to generation through poems, songs, myths, and legends.

Experts believe that the first inhabitants of southern Nigeria were nomads who lived by hunting and gathering wild foods. By A.D. 500 these early peoples had learned how to work iron, which they used to make farming tools and weapons for hunting. The invention of farming tools meant they were no longer forced to wander in search of food. They could now stay in one place. As a result of this development, the region's first settlements were founded.

EARLY SETTLEMENTS

Each settlement was made up of a clan or lineage, people who were all from the same family line, related to a common ancestor. The religion of the region focused on reverence of ancestors. If the people remembered and respected their ancestors, it was believed, the ancestors would watch over them and protect them.

The population of the region grew as farming techniques improved and more food was produced. Small settlements soon turned into villages, each inhabited by several different clans. Scholars believe that by the 1100s many people lived in villages, each of which was ruled by a council of elders. The council ensured that the community followed the laws and maintained the religious beliefs of the village. High earthen walls

The remains of the walls of Benin City date to around 1100.

enclosed each village, providing security and an added sense of unity.

As the population continued to grow, so did competition for land and resources. To face these new challenges, it appears that several villages often banded together.

In the area around Benin City, archaeologists have discovered a vast, interconnected network of earthen walls that date to around 1100. By that time, the region's villages were already joining forces, but they had not yet come together to form a single state. There was not yet a kingdom with one center or one ruler who was recognized by all.

IN THE LAND OF THE SKY KINGS

It is not known how and when the first king ruled over the region. According to Edo oral histories, Benin was first ruled by the *Ogiso*, which means "sky kings."

Who the Ogiso were and how long they ruled is also not known. We do know that they were not able to maintain their hold on power. For reasons not mentioned in Edo oral accounts, the population rebelled against the Ogiso and removed them from the throne.

The task of finding new rulers for the kingdom was given to the *uzama* (oo-zah-mah), a group of Edo chiefs. In search of a new king, the *uzama* turned for help to *Ife* (EE-fay), a powerful Yoruba kingdom. In response to the *uzama*'s request, it is believed, the king of Ife sent them his son *Oranmiyan*, a young man said to be part man and part god.

Oranmiyan married an Edo woman. Their son,

11

Edo chiefs continue to play an important role in Benin City. Chief I. Obasoyen wears ceremonial dress, including coral beads, a brass mask attached to his belt, and an *eben*, or ceremonial sword.

Eweka I, became king of Benin in about 1300. This was the beginning of the dynasty, or line of kings, that still rules Benin City today.

The descendants of the *uzama*, too, continue to play an important political and cultural role in Benin City.

THE ORANMIYAN DYNASTY

Eweka I and the two kings who followed him found themselves in constant conflict with the *uzama*. The *uzama*, hereditary chiefs present in Benin long before the arrival of Oranmiyan, were seen by many as representatives of the people. They spoke for the original Edo inhabitants of the kingdom—the vast majority of its citizens.

The kings were seen by the people, at least in part, as outsiders. Thus they competed with the *uzama*. This resulted in great tension between the two groups.

In time, the kingdom developed a complex system of checks and balances that allowed the kings and the *uzama* to rule together in relative peace. Before this could happen, however, several changes were made. The first of these was put in

Carved around A.D. 1100, this lovely clay head is a fine example of work created by artists in the powerful kingdom of Ife.

place by King Ewedo, the fourth ruler in the dynasty begun by Oranmiyan.

INCREASING THE KING'S POWER

Ewedo was the first king in the Oranmiyan dynasty to assert the full power of his position. In a famous battle that took place in the late 1300s—and is still celebrated today—he took over the central part of the Edo kingdom. There he built a palace and a town around it. The palace and the capital of the Benin kings still stand on this very spot in the heart of Benin City. Following his victory, Ewedo introduced new laws that took some power away from the *uzama*. This move strengthened his ability to rule and increased the power of the royal family.

One of Ewedo's descendants, King Ewuare, reigned in the mid-1400s. He too expanded the powers of the king. Ewuare passed laws that decreased the power of the *uzama* and increased the authority of the palace. Though anger between the two groups continued to flare occasionally, from this time forward it became clear that the king was the supreme authority in the land.

The leopard on this brass plaque from Benin is a symbol of the king's supreme power, which Ewuare helped establish.

Ewuare's reforms transformed the kingdom. This set the stage for a period of great glory, wealth, and military expansion for the kingdom—Benin's golden age.

2 OBA EWUARE

The Edo word for king is *oba* (OH-buh). In the eyes of his people, the *oba* was divine. Like Oranmiyan, the *oba* was considered part man and part god.

The *oba* was thought to act on behalf of his ancestors, mighty spirits who controlled the kingdom's fate. Each *oba,* it was said, was chosen by the gods, linked to heaven. He was seen as a source of life and fertility. Among his allies were powerful deities—such as *Olokun,* the sea god, provider of wealth and children. But the *oba* was also a source of death, because he alone could call for a person's execution.

FAMOUS OBAS

Eweka I	Came to power around A. D. 1300
Ewedo	Ruled in the late 1300s
Ewuare	Ruled in the mid-1400s
Ozolua	Ruled in the late 1400s
Esegie	Ruled in the early 1500s
Ewuakpe	Ruled in the late 1600s
Akenzua I	Ruled in the early 1700s
Eresonyen	Ruled in the mid-1700s
Ovoranmwen	Ruled in the late 1800s. Removed from the throne by the British
Eweka II	Ruled from 1914 to 1933
Akenzua II	Ruled from 1933 to 1978
Erediauwa	Present ruler who came to power in 1978

The *oba* inserted these brass figures into the ground at his side when judging important legal cases.

An English visitor to Benin in the 1700s commented on the *oba*'s great spiritual power:

> The King of Benin occupies a higher post here than the Pope does in Catholic Europe; . . . he is not only God's [representative] on Earth, but a god himself, whose subjects both adore and obey him.

OBA EWUARE AND HIS CAPITAL

When Ewuare came to power in the mid-1400s, he redesigned and enlarged the capital founded by his ancestor Ewedo.

Ewuare borrowed the city plan used by the Yoruba people of Ife. The plan consisted of a series of roads radiating outward from the central palace, like spokes from the center of a wheel. Using adobe brick, a material favored by the rulers of Ife, he built a thick and imposing wall that enclosed the city. The wall was 24 miles (38 km) around.

The palace area, too, was surrounded by a wall, which created a private enclosure for the king, a royal city within the city. This second wall set the *oba* apart and emphasized Oba Ewuare's status and power. It also separated him from the *uzama*, whose quarters stood several miles west of the palace.

The king's inner city was divided in half by a wide road. On one side, called *Ogbe*, was the *ogbe* or palace, along with the quarters of the *oba*'s most trusted allies, titleholders belonging to an organization called *Eghaevbo n' Ogbe*. On the other side,

Ore (meaning "town"), lived the Town Chiefs, titleholders associated with an organization called *Eghaevbo n' Ore.*

The Ogbe titleholders managed the details of palace life. They oversaw the *oba*'s cooks and pages, guarded his many wives and children, supervised all artists and craftsmen working for the king, met with foreign traders, and cared for the ruler's clothes, ceremonial garments, and jewelry.

The Ore chiefs administered Benin's outlying territories. They were the kingdom's tax collectors, military recruiters, and, most important, the primary link between the *oba* and his people.

Unlike the title of *oba* or *uzama,* both of which were passed down from father to son, titles in Eghaevbo n' Ogbe and Eghaevbo n' Ore could not be inherited. They had to be earned. This made it impossible for any one person or lineage to become too powerful, a state of affairs that suited the *oba* well. But it did not prevent conflicts from erupting in the capital. Anger often flared between the Eghaevbo n' Ogbe and Eghaevbo n' Ore, sometimes resulting in violent clashes.

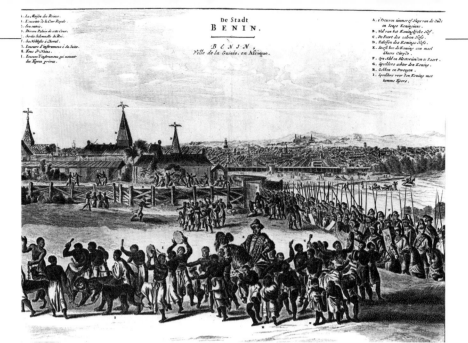

This drawing of Benin City, published in 1668, shows the *oba* on horseback surrounded by warriors, musicians, dwarfs, and leopards. In the background is the palace, which has large turrets and is separated from the rest of the city by a wall.

No one knows exactly what Ewuare's capital looked like. However, Europeans who visited Benin in the 1500s and 1600s recorded some of their observations.

Dutch sailors who traveled to Benin in the 1600s were impressed. They noted that the city had long, straight avenues, thirty in all, each 120 feet (37 m) wide. The *oba*'s inner city, they reported, was as large as the city of Haarlem in the Netherlands. They saw five galleries "as broad as the galleries at the stock exchange in Amsterdam," their roofs supported by pillars, as well as several gateways, courtyards, audience chambers, and meeting halls. The sailors noted that the city's buildings were "polished and shining like a mirror," and they praised its "good laws" and "well-organized police." Atop the main gates of the palace were massive birds and snakes made of brass, symbols of the *oba*'s power.

A BELOVED *OBA*

Of the many *obas* who are remembered in Benin today, Ewuare remains one of the most beloved. Apart from redesigning the city and palace and changing the way the kingdom was ruled, Ewuare was a great soldier. Heading the army himself, he conquered lands far to the west and east, bringing under his command peoples long ruled by Yoruba monarchs in the west and Igbo chiefs in the east. Many of the ceremonies celebrated today at the Benin court were introduced by Ewuare, who was also a great supporter of the arts.

3 THE WARRIOR KINGS

Ewuare's successor, his son Ozolua, was also a great warrior. Under his command in the late 1400s, Benin continued to expand.

Wherever he won a victory, Ozolua sent one of his sons to rule the conquered territory. In some cases, this strategy was very effective, ensuring the loyalty of distant provinces. In other instances, it was a failure. Some outlying areas refused to submit to the *oba*. Their citizens rebelled against the central authority of Benin City, causing unrest along the kingdom's outer edges.

Other areas agreed only to partial submission. That was the case in many Edo villages. In those communities, it was common to find two leaders: an envoy (*onogie*) sent by the *oba* and a local leader (*odionwere*) chosen by the community for his wisdom and experience.

Such Edo villages also had their own social structure, which was completely different from the structure of the royal capital. Instead of titleholders, the villages had age-grade associations, organizations that grouped together men of the same age. Each age grade was entrusted with certain tasks, such as road construction and building repair, community policing, and legal matters. The *odionwere* oversaw the entire age-grade system and acted as the village priest.

During King Ozolua's reign, Europeans first arrived in Benin. Sailors sent by King John II of Portugal reached Benin between 1472 and 1486.

ESEGIE AND THE EUROPEANS

Ozolua's son Esegie was also a warrior who ruled Benin in the early 1500s. He is remembered for two battles he fought: a bloody conflict with his brother for control of the throne, and a war he almost lost against *Idah*, a powerful *city-state*

Brass plaque showing Portuguese visitors to Benin City

100 miles (161 km) northeast of Benin City. He also established strong ties with the Portuguese.

During Oba Esegie's reign, Benin's relationship with Portugal blossomed. The Portuguese brought cloth, coral beads, and brass in the form of *manillas*, horseshoe-shaped brass objects that were a common form of currency in the 1500s. These goods were all used to make court regalia—the clothing, furnishings, and ornaments of royalty.

In exchange, the Portuguese received ivory, pepper, cloth made by Edo weavers, and slaves. In the early 1500s the *obas* stopped exporting slaves because they needed their labor in the kingdom.

The Portuguese did not seek to colonize Benin. Instead, they set up a partnership with the kingdom. This partnership was based on trade and military ties. In fact, some Portuguese soldiers served in the armies of Oba Esegie.

GROWTH OF POWER

Just as the Portuguese soldiers were used to strengthen the *oba*'s armies, so too their presence was used to reinforce the people's belief in the *oba*'s links with the spirit world. The tremendous

Portuguese soldiers, such as the one shown in this sculpture, fought for Oba Esegie.

wealth reaped by the court from its trade with Portugal was said to be a gift from Olokun, the sea deity, to the *oba,* his representative on earth.

Thanks to the wealth and spiritual prestige brought about by Esegie's ties to the Portuguese and to Benin's increased military strength, the court gained great power.

4 RENEWAL AND DECLINE

By the 1600s Benin was having a difficult time. Relations between the palace and the titleholders living in the *oba*'s city began to deteriorate. Soon they went from bad to worse. Territories were lost, and money was spent foolishly. Princes competed for the throne throughout the late 1600s and waged battles over it. In the early 1700s a terrible civil war was fought in Benin.

BENIN EMERGES ANEW

The Kingdom of Benin began to regain its former stature only in the mid-1700s. Two kings played an important role in bringing about this renewal:

Oba Akenzua and his son Eresonyen. Both established new commercial ties with Europe, especially with the Netherlands. In the 1700s, Benin again entered the slave trade.

The *obas* who ruled from the late 1700s to the mid-1800s were tremendously wealthy. Unlike their predecessors, however, they were neither great warriors nor great traders. They did not look outward but inward, concentrating instead on court rituals and regalia. Under them, the arts flourished, reflecting the kingdom's wealth.

By the mid-1800s, trade with Europe began to falter. European merchants started trading with other peoples in the Niger Delta to the south. Benin began to lose its privileged position in the commerce between Europe and Africa.

Benin's relationships with other foreign powers also began to suffer. Among those others were Nupe, a Muslim state to the north, and Great Britain, which had replaced Portugal and the Netherlands as the main European nation trading in the region.

By the end of the 1800s, disagreements with the British over trade had led to violent conflict.

British officers sit among objects looted from the palace in Benin City. When the British burned the capital, they stole many of Benin's treasures.

THE DESTRUCTION OF THE KINGDOM

Oba Ovoranmwen came to power in 1888. Nine years later, in 1897, he was removed from the throne. Benin City was looted and destroyed by British troops. Without a leader, the kingdom of Benin fell.

The British did not wish to see the kingdom disappear but did want to have it under their control. Years later, they put Ovoranmwen's son Eweka II on the throne, thinking he would be easy to manipulate.

Although he was forced to work closely with the British, Eweka II was resourceful. He successfully rebuilt and restored key aspects of the kingship.

5 THE ARTS OF BENIN

The Benin Kingdom is best known today for its beautiful arts. Examples of these arts are found in the world's leading museums.

The *obas* used art as a political tool to reinforce their power, rather than purely for decoration. Art showed the king's wealth. It pointed to the king's political and spiritual powers and emphasized his nature as part human, part god.

Works of art conveyed these ideas in a number of ways. The subject of each work, the way in which the work was used, the symbols included in it, and the materials from which it was made all had meaning.

BRASS AND IVORY

Only the king and some of his nobles were allowed to own art objects made from certain materials, particularly brass and ivory. Brass and ivory were both associated with the powerful sea god, Olokun.

Brass is a mixture of two metals, copper and zinc. It was considered sacred in Benin because its shininess reminded the Edo of the spirit world, called *Erinmwin*. The unusual red-gold color of copper and the tremendous heat required to melt it before making works of art were both regarded as extraordinary. These qualities were reminders of the awesome powers of Olokun and of his representative on earth, the *oba*, both of whom could behave as furiously as a raging fire.

Ivory, smooth and creamy white, was seen as a cool and soothing substance, a perfect counterpart to the fiery nature of brass. Associated with purity, ivory was a reminder of the life-giving power of Olokun and the similar role of his representative, the *oba*, as a spiritual source of fertility.

Members of Igun Eronmwon make brass sculptures using the lost wax method. First, sculptures are modeled in wax (above). The figures are then cased in a clay mold and fired, causing the wax to melt and disappear. Molten bronze is poured into the resulting mold, filling the spaces left by the wax and creating a bronze sculpture.

ARTISTS

Only artists appointed by the court could work with brass or ivory. These artists belonged to associations called guilds, which were founded and overseen by the *oba*. The brass workers' guild, *Igun Eronmwon*, was probably founded by King Ewuare or his grandson King Esegie. The guild of ivory carvers, *Igbesanmwan*, was created, it is said, under the Ogiso kings.

Members of both these guilds worked in the *oba*'s inner city. Each guild was highly organized, with several grades, an apprenticeship system, masters and students, titleholders, and religious officials. Membership was passed from father to son.

Most of the art objects made by the guilds were used in the palace. Many were displayed during ceremonies honoring the *oba*. Others served a religious purpose. They were placed on altars to celebrate and strengthen the king's links with the spirit world. Still others were used to decorate the palace. Often, a single work of art played several roles: as an object of beauty, a religious icon, and a symbol of the *oba*'s political power. Many such objects also recalled important historical events.

OBA HEADS

The Edo remembered their past rulers by setting up altars to honor them. In the culture of Benin, the *oba*'s head is regarded as the place where all his spiritual power is concentrated.

According to Edo oral history, it was the

This bronze head of an *oba* once stood in a shrine honoring royal ancestors.

custom to cut off the heads of Benin kings after they died and send the heads to Ife. Ife, which was renowned for making beautiful brass sculptures, sent a brass head representing the dead king back to Benin. This practice was followed until the reign of Ozolua in the late 1400s. Oba Ozolua asked Ife to send an artist to Benin City to teach Edo craftsmen how to make bronze heads. Ife sent a man named Igueghae, who taught the *oba*'s brasscasters this important skill.

Some scholars believe that this account is a myth, created to emphasize the close ties between

An altar in the *oba*'s palace, with brass heads and carved ivory tusks

Ife and Benin, and others believe it is historically accurate.

It is known that from the mid-1400s on, when Ewuare ruled, life-size brass heads depicting deceased *obas* were placed in shrines located in the palace. The heads were not portraits but idealized images. They represented the *oba* not as a real person but as a perfect, divine being.

The brass heads were hollow. At the top was a circular opening into which an elephant tusk was placed. Reaching toward the sky, the tusk may have symbolized the king's links with heaven. Such head-and-tusk combinations are still seen on altars in the palace today.

OBA FIGURES

The Edo placed brass figures of the king dressed in court attire on palace altars alongside the *oba* heads. These brass *oba* figures reveal a great deal about the wealth of the kingdom.

In a figure made in the 1800s, for instance, the *oba* wears a bulky skirt and many royal ornaments made of red coral, a costly material first imported by Ewuare. Coral beads adorn the king's headdress, collar, chest, upper arms, wrists, and ankles. Over his skirt hangs a brass pendant shaped like a ram's head. Pendants of this kind, some made of ivory, others of brass, were among the finest works produced for Benin kings.

In each hand, the *oba* carries an item associated with kingship. In his left hand is a royal proclamation staff, much like a scepter. In his right hand is an *eben*, a type of sword carried by the *oba* and title-holders during ceremonies.

Today, such regalia can still be seen at court ceremonies in Benin City.

By the early 1500s, manillas supplied by Portuguese traders were used to create the brass *oba* figures, *oba* heads, trophy heads, and queen-mother heads placed on palace altars. An 18-inch (45-cm) brass plaque from the Benin court shows Portuguese men and manillas.

This bronze head is believed to depict an enemy ruler captured by the *oba*'s army in the 1300s.

TROPHY HEADS AND QUEEN-MOTHER HEADS

Brass heads were placed on two other types of altars within the palace as well: altars celebrating warfare and altars honoring the king's mother.

After a Benin victory in battle, the heads of enemy rulers were cut off. The heads were brought to the palace, where court artists cast them in brass. These castings, known as trophy heads, were placed in a war shrine called *Aro-Okuo*. Trophy heads were probably introduced during the period of warfare and expansion that marked the reigns of kings Ewuare, Ozolua, and Esegie.

Oral history recalls that Esegie managed to defeat the city-state of Idah only with the help of his mother, Idia, a skilled military leader. For her, Esegie created a new title, *Iyoba*, meaning queen mother. From Esegie's reign onward, altars and brass heads were made in honor of queen mothers.

Like *oba* heads, queen-mother heads were idealized images. They showed the king's mother as a perfect being, crowned with an elaborate, coral-covered headdress.

Brass sculpture of a queen mother from the sixteenth century

PALACE PLAQUES

By Esegie's reign, the palace had become a magnificent treasury of arts. The pillars in its galleries

The *oba* and members of the court wore fine pendants of ivory and brass, such as these made in the seventeenth century.

were covered with brass plaques—book-sized sheets of brass that depicted complex scenes. The plaques emphasized the wealth and tremendous power of the *oba*, often showing him surrounded by allies, servants, and objects of beauty.

Brass was an expensive material in the Benin region. In the kingdom's early years, brass was

Ivory container from the late sixteenth century showing two Portuguese soldiers fighting beside a dragon. The carver from Benin based the dragon on a European image of a dragon.

imported from within Africa. By the time Esegie was *oba*, it was being supplied by Portuguese traders. The wealth that the court derived from trade with the Portuguese is reflected in the images on palace plaques. Many plaques show Portuguese merchants with long, straight hair. The Portuguese figures often hold manillas, the form in which brass was traded in the 1500s.

IVORY ART

Apart from the elaborately decorated elephant tusks that were inserted into brass *oba* heads, many other types of objects were carved in ivory for use by the royal court. Delicate figures of kings and queens were made of ivory, too, as well as fine pendants and bracelets that were worn by members of the court.

Fine works in ivory were made for sale to the Portuguese in the late 1400s and the early 1500s. Among these were lidded containers, drinking vessels, spoons, and knife handles, each decorated with beautifully carved figures. The carvings included images of Portuguese soldiers and knights, European children, angels, animals, and boats. In these pieces, Edo carvers created a completely new kind of art, unlike anything that they or any European craftsmen had ever produced. Some of these works, bought by kings and queens in Europe, can be seen today in museums.

In the 1600s the Dutch replaced the Portuguese as the main European traders in the Benin region. The Dutch were particularly interested in ivory, and by the mid-1700s, trade in this precious material was booming.

During the mid- to late 1700s, Benin artists created stunning ivory carvings. Exquisite ivory locks were made for the palace. Altars to honor past kings were decorated with finely carved tusks and beautiful leopard figures—symbols of the king's overwhelming economic, physical, and spiritual power.

In the late 1700s, Britain became Benin's main trading partner. British visitors to the kingdom during this time described and sketched some of the many kings' altars at the palace. On nearly all of these altars they saw intricately carved elephant tusks.

STOLEN TREASURES

In 1897 British troops entered Benin City. They removed Oba Ovoranmwen and destroyed the capital. Large sections of the palace were looted and set on fire. Thousands of works of art were seized and shipped to Europe. Most were turned over to British museums. Many pieces remained in England; others were sold to museums throughout Europe and, later, the United States.

Many of the works that were looted had been altarpieces, sacred objects created to celebrate the spirits of deceased rulers. As a result, this theft of the treasures of Benin, which Europeans had so admired for centuries, was also an offense against the religious beliefs of the kingdom.

ARTISTIC REBIRTH

Oba Ovoranmwen was exiled by the British to the port city of Calabar, in southern Nigeria, where he died.

For more than fifteen years the Kingdom of Benin was without a ruler. Finally, in 1914 Oba Eweka II was enthroned by the British. Eweka rebuilt the royal residence and invited court artists, who had fled the capital, to return to Benin City and create new works to replace those looted by the British. He displayed these new works on a single altar, which he dedicated to all of his predecessors. Thanks to him and his followers, whom he inspired, Benin City remains today an important center of political, religious, and artistic expression.

When Eweka died in 1933, a large altar was built in his honor. Later, additional altars were built for each of the kings who had ruled since 1850. These can still be seen in the palace today.

During his lifetime Eweka had allowed the court artists to sell their works to *commoners* and

In the twentieth century, artists in Benin began to experiment with new forms of art, such as these clay sculptures on the walls of Benin City.

foreigners. This encouraged the artists to develop new styles and types of objects. Under Eweka's son Akenzua II, who ruled from 1933 to 1978, artists in the capital experimented with novel ideas and forms. Drawing on the tradition of brass plaques popular in Esegie's time, Akenzua called on a famous artist named Ovia Idah to create clay plaques for the palace walls. The *oba* also encouraged his daughter Princess Elizabeth Olowo to begin making works in brass and wood, materials that only men had been allowed to use in the kingdom up to that time.

The current king, Oba Erediauwa, is a lawyer trained at Oxford University in England. He is a dedicated patron of the arts. Under his rule, carving, brass work, beadwork, and textile design continue to flourish.

6 BENIN'S LEGACY

Today Benin City is a thriving urban center, home to 250,000 people. It has several colleges, including the University of Benin, and many rubber factories.

Although the Kingdom of Benin is no longer an independent state, the *oba* and his palace are still the heart and soul of the Edo community. Many Edo live outside the city—throughout Nigeria, in other African countries, in Europe, and in the United States—but most think of Benin City as their home and consider the *oba* their spiritual leader.

This is most clearly evident during annual celebrations held in Benin City. In the past, ceremonies celebrating the *oba*, his court, and his ancestors were

Many Edo who live abroad still consider Benin City—with its rich court traditions, annual celebrations, and art—their home. Above, an Edo chief participates in a celebration.

Chief Ize Iyamu in ceremonial attire. Benin's proud traditions are celebrated at court ceremonies, when the *oba*, chiefs, and officials appear in full regalia.

held at regular intervals throughout the year, sometimes for months on end. Today they are held during a ten-day period at Christmastime, when most Nigerians have time off from work.

CELEBRATIONS

The two most important celebrations, introduced by Oba Ewuare, are *Ugie Erha Oba*, which celebrates the king's ancestors, and *Igue*, which serves to honor the king and renew his semidivine powers.

Ugie Erha Oba begins with a community celebration. Throughout Benin, families commemorate their fathers' ancestors. At the palace, each of the *oba*'s forefathers is honored individually. Particular attention is paid to the king's father.

All the city's chiefs and titleholders respectfully greet the ruling *oba* during a special ceremony that emphasizes the *oba*'s role as supreme leader of Benin. The king then dances in public, dressed in an exquisite, crimson-colored wrap and elaborate coral ornaments. Surrounded by attendants, he oversees the placement of gifts on the altar that honors his father. The festival ends with a theatrical mock battle recalling the reign of Ewuare, in which contemporary descendants of the *uzama* fight men loyal to the *oba*. The *oba*'s supporters win, demonstrating the *oba*'s power.

The high point of the second celebration, Igue, is a series of rites in which plant substances are applied to the king's body to strengthen him for the coming year. Animals are sacrificed to honor the *oba*'s head and his spiritual power. At the end of Igue, the king, draped in elegant cloth and sounding an ivory gong, dances to purify the city.

Under the current ruler, Oba Erediauwa, many other celebrations that were stopped after the British invasion are being revived. During the ceremonies, older works of art created many decades ago and new works made in recent years are presented side by side. Together, they reveal the stunning beauty of the Benin court and demonstrate its long and proud heritage. These works of art underscore the continuing importance of the Kingdom of Benin as a center of culture: a place that encourages new ideas while treasuring its history and the richness of its past.

TIMELINE

A.D. c. 500	Nomadic peoples of southern Nigeria learn to forge iron
c. 1000	Nomadic groups settle in clusters, then in villages
c. 1300	Eweka becomes *oba*
late 1300s	Oba Ewedo claims greater authority over *uzama* and builds capital, Edo, and first palace
mid-1400s	Oba Ewuare establishes *oba*'s authority over *uzama*; rebuilds and reorganizes capital and palace; conquers vast new territories; and introduces new art forms and rituals
late 1400s	Oba Ozolua conquers new territory; first contact with Portuguese
early 1500s	Oba Esegie conquers new territory and establishes strong trade relations with Portuguese
early 1700s	Akenzua I rebuilds the formerly declining power of the monarchy and wealth of the kingdom
mid-1700s	Eresonyen continues growth of royal power and prosperity
late 1800s	Increasing tension with Great Britain
1897	British troops invade, loot, and burn capital; Oba Ovoranmwen is exiled
1914	Eweka II becomes *oba*; he rebuilds palace and restores some royal traditions
1933	Oba Akenzua II comes to power
1978	Oba Erediauwa comes to power

GLOSSARY

Aro-Okuo palace shrine dedicated to war victories

city-state a state that is made up of a city and its surrounding territory

commoner a person who is not of royal or noble rank

court regalia emblems or decorations that indicate close association with the palace

eben ceremonial sword

Edo people who form the majority of the Kingdom of Benin's inhabitants; original name of the Kingdom of Benin and of Benin City

Eghaevbo n'Ogbe association of titleholders who administered the king's palace and were the king's closest allies

Eghaevbo n'Ore association of titleholders who administered Benin's outlying regions

Erinmwin spirit world

Idah powerful city-state north of Benin City

Ife powerful Yoruba kingdom; birthplace of Oranmiyan; an important center of culture that greatly influenced the culture of much of southeastern Nigeria

Igbesanmwan ivory carvers' guild in Benin City

Igue annual festival held to strengthen the king's powers

Igun Eronmwon brass workers' guild in Benin City

Iyoba Edo word for queen mother

manillas horseshoe-shaped brass ingots used as currency

oba Edo word for king

Ogbe Edo word for palace; side of the king's inner city where officials responsible for palace administration lived

Ogiso sky kings; first ruling dynasty in Edo region

Olokun god of the sea; source of wealth and children

Oranmiyan semidivine son of the ruler of Ife sent to Benin

Ore Edo word for town; side of the king's inner city where officials responsible for issues beyond the palace lived

Ugie Erha Oba annual festival held to honor fathers' ancestors and power of the *oba*

uzama council of Edo chiefs

FOR FURTHER READING

Azuone, Chukwuma. *Edo: The Bini People of the Benin Kingdom*. New York: Rosen Publishing Group, 1996.
Encyclopaedia Britannica CD-ROM Version 1997. Articles on "African Arts," "Benin," "Benin City," "Edo," "Western Africa."
Koslow, Philip. *Benin: Lords of the River*. New York: Chelsea House, 1995.

FOR ADVANCED READERS
Ben-Amos, Paula. *The Art of Benin*, rev. ed. Washington, DC, and London: Smithsonian Institution Press and British Museum Press, 1995.
Blackmun, Barbara. "The Elephant and Its Ivory in Benin." In *Elephant: The Animal and Its Ivory in African Culture*, edited by Doran Ross. Los Angeles: Fowler Museum of Cultural History/University of California Press, 1992.

Drewal, Henry, John Pemberton III, and Rowland Abiodun. *Yoruba: Nine Centuries of African Art and Thought.* New York: Center for African Art/Harry N. Abrams, Inc., 1989.

Ezra, Kate. *Royal Art of Benin.* New York: Metropolitan Museum of Art/Harry N. Abrams, Inc., 1992.

Freyer, Bryna. *Royal Benin Art in the Collection of the National Museum of African Art.* Washington, DC, and London: Smithsonian Institution Press, 1987.

Vogel, Susan, ed. *Africa and the Renaissance: Art in Ivory.* New York: Center for African Art/Prestel-Verlag, 1988.

WEB SITES

Due to the changeable nature of the Internet, sites appear and disappear very quickly. Internet addresses must be entered with capital and lowercase letters exactly as they appear.

Africa South of the Sahara:
http://www-sul.stanford.edu/depts/ssrg/africa/guide.html

H-AFRICA Home Page: http://h-net.msu.edu/~africa/

Nigeria.Com: http://www.nigeria.com

Nigeria Page: http://www.sas.upenn.edu/African_Studies/Country_Specific/Nigeria.html

Nigerian Information Resources Online:
http://www.coe.uncc.edu/~ecodili/nigeria.html

INDEX

ACKNOWLEDGMENTS

The work of several scholars, all of whom have studied at length the arts of Benin, was of great help in writing these pages. A debt of gratitude is due, in particular, to Paula Girshick Ben-Amos, Barbara Blackmun, Kate Ezra, and Bryna Freyer for their publications. I am, as always, grateful to Bart Legum for his patience and the keen eye that he casts upon my words. To Bert Orlov, many thanks as well.

ABOUT THE AUTHOR

Dominique Malaquais holds a doctorate in Africanist art history from Columbia University. She has taught, lectured, and published extensively on the arts and architecture of sub-Saharan Africa in the United States, Europe, and Africa. In addition, she has mounted several exhibitions of African art. The author lives in New York City and teaches at Princeton University.